LUNGEING

by
Judy Harvey FBHS

Illustrations by
Carole Vincer

KENILWORTH PRESS

First published in the UK in 1996
by Kenilworth Press, an imprint of Quiller Publishing Ltd

Reprinted 1997, 1999, 2002, 2003, 2006, 2008, 2012

British Library Cataloguing-in-Publication Data
    A catalogue record for this book
    is available from the British Library

ISBN 978 1 872082 82 0

Printed in China

Kenilworth Press

An imprint of Quiller Publishing Ltd
Wykey House, Wykey, Shrewsbury, SY4 1JA
Tel: 01939 261616 Fax: 01939 261606
E-mail: info@quillerbooks.com
Website: www.kenilworthpress.co.uk

CONTENTS

Introduction

Lungeing can be a highly beneficial means of training and exercising a horse. Safe and effective lungeing is a skill which requires practice – if carried out incorrectly, it can be dangerous for both horse and handler. You will certainly find it much easier to master the techniques if you learn using a horse that already knows the work and is easy to lunge.

Lungeing is an indispensable part of the unbroken horse's **early training**. It teaches him obedience and develops rhythmic paces, building up the correct muscles. It teaches him to accept the bit and provides a means of control when he is first backed and ridden.

Lungeing is useful in the **retraining** of a horse which has developed bad habits. It persuades him to go in a correct outline without having to cope with the additional problem of balancing with the rider's weight.

When time is short, lungeing can provide useful **exercise**. If the horse is over-fresh, lungeing can help to settle him, getting rid of any excessive high spirits before the rider gets on.

Early **jumping** work carried out on the lunge is useful when assessing a horse's ability and developing his technique.

Skilled lungeing, in expert hands, can provide '**physiotherapy**' to relieve muscle problems in the back and hind legs.

The lungeing area

It is essential that lungeing is carried out on a safe, level surface. The strain of turning continually is considerable and injuries may occur if the going is unsuitable – e.g. deep and holding, hard or slippery. Good grass is fine but you will very quickly wear a permanent track if you lunge on the same area too often.

Unless you are very experienced and know your horse well, always lunge in a confined area. It is quite easy to 'fence off' a quiet corner in a field using jump poles and wings; just make sure that the 'fence' is high enough and appears solid. The area should be a minimum of 20m x 20m.

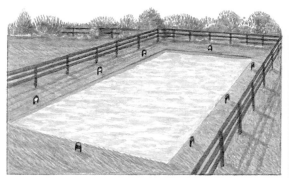

Equipment

The **lunge rein** should be made from tubular webbing with a strong leather strap to attach it to the cavesson or bit. Nylon lunge reins should not be used – they slip and can burn your hands, even through gloves.

Some lunge reins have a metal clip to attach to the cavesson. These tend to bang on the horse's nose and can bend out of shape.

A plain **snaffle bridle** should be used. The noseband and the reins can be taken off to make it less bulky, unless the horse is going to be ridden immediately after he has been lunged.

Protect the horse's legs with **brushing boots** or carefully fitted bandages. **Overreach boots** are essential if jumping.

The **whip** needs to be long enough to be able to touch the horse with the lash when he is out on a big circle. The problem here is that long whips can be cumbersome and unbalanced, so try to choose one you can manage comfortably. Experienced horses very quickly get to know how long a whip is and learn to stay just out of reach!

Gloves are essential to protect your hands and to prevent the lunge rein from slipping. Any riding glove with which you are comfortable is suitable.

It is sensible to wear a hard **hat**. The horse may rear or kick out and a hat can prevent a serious injury.

A **lungeing roller** is similar to a normal roller except that it has rings for attaching side-reins at different heights. These rings may also be used when long-reining.

The roller can be used to introduce a young unbroken horse to a saddle. It is more convenient to use a roller rather than a saddle, if the horse is not going to be ridden afterwards. If the horse has a

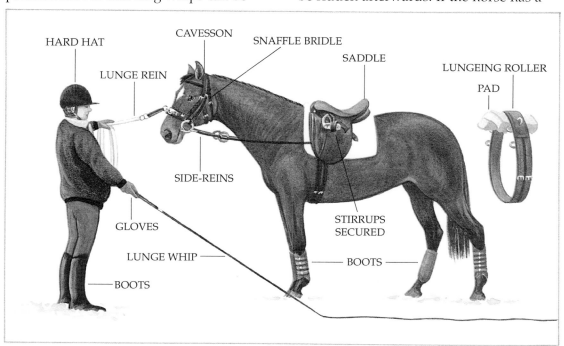

HARD HAT

CAVESSON

SNAFFLE BRIDLE

SADDLE

LUNGEING ROLLER

LUNGE REIN

PAD

SIDE-REINS

STIRRUPS SECURED

GLOVES

LUNGE WHIP

BOOTS

BOOTS

Equipment (continued)

sore back, a roller may not come into contact with the problem area; the horse can then be kept fit with correct lungeing whilst allowing the back to heal.

When fitting a roller it is a good idea to use a breastplate to prevent it slipping back. This is essential with young horses as you will not be able to tighten up the girth fully at first. Use padding under the roller to prevent pressure on the horse's spine or withers.

The **lunge cavesson** is a thickly padded noseband, reinforced with metal, with rings on the front for attaching the lunge rein. Only the central ring should be used.

The cavesson should be fitted with great care. If it is too loose the cheekpiece can be pulled into the horse's eye and there will be too much movement on the nose, causing discomfort.

Some cavessons can be fitted as 'drop' nosebands, useful when lungeing a strong horse.

Lungeing a horse with the lunge rein attached direct to the bit requires a lot of skill. It is very difficult to maintain a contact which is elastic enough to prevent permanent damage to the mouth. It should only be done when the horse is over-fresh or very strong and likely to get out of control.

A **saddle** is required if the horse is also to be ridden and to attach the side-reins to if a roller is not available. The stirrups must be tied up securely. A surcingle over the saddle will prevent the flaps blowing up and frightening a young horse.

Side-reins encourage the horse to seek the bit and to work in a correct outline with actively engaged hind legs. They are **not** used to 'pull the horse's head in'. Plain leather side-reins are the best, or those with a 'rubber ring' insert. Elasticated side-reins tend to have too

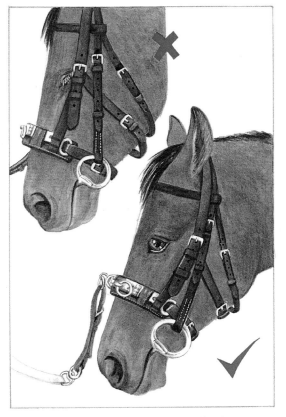

The cavesson noseband must be high enough not to pinch the skin around the bit. The cheek strap needs to be done up tightly to prevent the cavesson pulling into the eye.

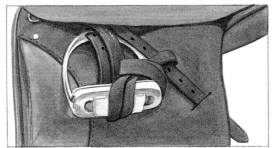

The stirrups are secured by passing the leather around the base of the stirrup and passing the spare end of the leather through the loop.

much play in them and can encourage the horse to snatch at the bit.

Side-reins usually buckle onto the girth or roller and have a spring clip at the other end to attach to the bit. The side-reins should be fitted at the same height, on either side of the horse. Always attach them to the girth first, clipping the free end onto the saddle or roller, until you are ready to use them. Never lead a horse with the side-reins clipped to the bit – he may feel the sudden restriction and panic.

When deciding on what length to fit the side-reins always be on the cautious side, fitting them a hole too long rather than a hole too tight. If fitting them for the first time, have them long enough that the horse only just makes contact with the bit when his neck is fully stretched. They should be the same length on each side. Once the horse accepts working forwards on the lunge into the side-reins, they can be shortened to help achieve the outline appropriate to his stage of training.

Walking for long periods with the side-reins done up is not recommended. The horse nods his head and neck in walk, but the side-reins inhibit this and can cause the walk to be restricted.

Start with the side-reins long enough for the horse to have a contact on his mouth when standing with his head in a natural position. Never force his head into position.

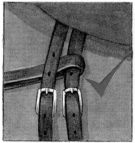

Attach the side-reins to the girth straps by threading them through the second strap and under the first. This will prevent them slipping down and help keep them level.

Twist the reins and thread the throat lash through the twists. This will keep them out of the way and prevent them from going over the horse's head.

Technique

Holding the lunge rein

There are several ways to do this, but the one outlined here is simple, efficient, and gives good control, both when lungeing on the flat and over fences. All methods require plenty of practice – try attaching the rein to a gate post and rehearsing the techniques.

Never use a lunge rein that someone else has coiled – always coil it yourself. Start off on the left rein – most horses are more co-operative this way. Stand on the horse's near side, hold the lunge rein close enough to his head to keep control with your left hand. Drop the rest of the lunge rein to the side, where neither you nor the horse will tread on it. Coil the rein up into your left hand; the loops should be small enough to keep clear of the ground, but large enough not to tighten around your hand. When you get to the end, hold the handle in your right hand and transfer the loops from your left hand, turning them over so that as the rein is let out the loops unravel from the top. Your left hand can now pay out or gather in the line without getting in a muddle. You will probably find it most comfortable to hold the rein between your third and little fingers as if you were riding. With practice this will take only seconds! When you change the rein, repeat the exercise, coiling the rein into your right hand, then transferring the loops to your left hand.

During this whole procedure you should keep the lunge whip under your arm, pointing it behind you so as not to frighten the horse.

Aids

We communicate with the horse on the lunge using the whip, lunge rein, voice and body position.

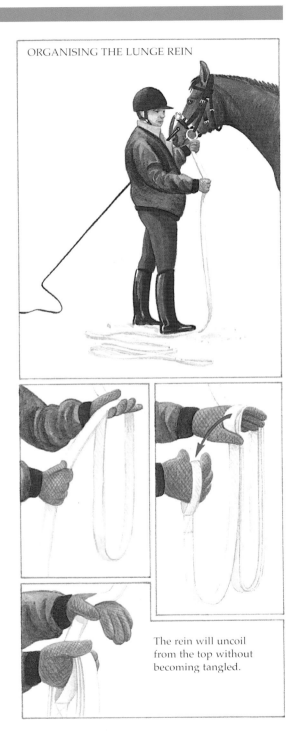

ORGANISING THE LUNGE REIN

The rein will uncoil from the top without becoming tangled.

Holding the lunge rein. *Left:* the loops are held in the whip hand; this makes it easier to adjust the rein. *Right:* this method is more suitable for experienced horses.

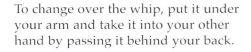

To change over the whip, put it under your arm and take it into your other hand by passing it behind your back.

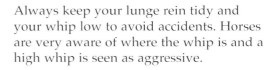

Always keep your lunge rein tidy and your whip low to avoid accidents. Horses are very aware of where the whip is and a high whip is seen as aggressive.

Technique (continued)

The **whip** sends the horse forwards when directed towards his hindquarters, and keeps him out on the circle when pointed towards his shoulder. When pointed at his ribs it will help create more bend. A 'touch' with the whip should be all that is necessary; it is usually enough just to 'flick' it towards him. Never 'crack' the whip when other horses are near by!

In the same way as when riding, the **rein contact** must be consistent and elastic, with the 'aids' given with the fingers. The horse can be asked to slow down or bend more to the inside. The rein is used in conjunction with the other aids.

Your tone of **voice** is important. Low and soft to slow down, higher pitched and sharper to go forward, e.g. 'Whoa-o-oh' or 'Trot-on'. Always use the same words of command.

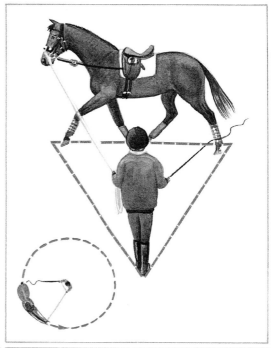

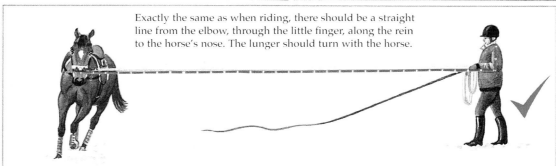

Exactly the same as when riding, there should be a straight line from the elbow, through the little finger, along the rein to the horse's nose. The lunger should turn with the horse.

To send the horse forwards, **position yourself** more towards his hindquarters; to slow him down, come level or in front of his eye. When he is going well, adopt a passive position level with the girth. You are the apex of a triangle, the horse is the base, the whip and rein the two sides.

Starting off

Lead the horse to the centre of the area where you are lungeing. Check all the tack, and make sure that your lunge rein is coiled correctly. If the horse is experienced and sensible, start him off without attaching the side-reins. This will help to get him thinking forward and any slight lameness will be more apparent. Begin on the left rein. Your whip and the coils of the lunge rein will be in your right hand. Stand level with his shoulder and, with the whip pointing down at his hind feet, ask him to 'walk on'. The fingers of your left hand should allow the lunge rein to slip through them as he walks forwards onto the circle. Walk with him until he is on a circle, gently keeping

him going forwards with the whip. Once he is on the circle you can ask him to 'trot on'. Get him out onto as large a circle as possible. Practise some transitions down into walk or halt and then forward again into trot. Never allow him to turn in towards you. Once you feel in control on the left rein, make him halt and then change over to the right rein. Make sure that your lunge rein is coiled correctly. Most horses are less keen to move off on the right rein and will try to face you. Move towards his hindquarters, but never close enough to be kicked, and send him forwards; make sure that you 'allow' him forward with your rein. Once he has been loosened up on both reins, you can then attach the side-reins to help him work in a correct outline. This will help to improve his muscular development and way of going. Attach the side-rein on the outside first – it will give you more control should he shoot off. Vary the work with transitions and frequent changes of rein.

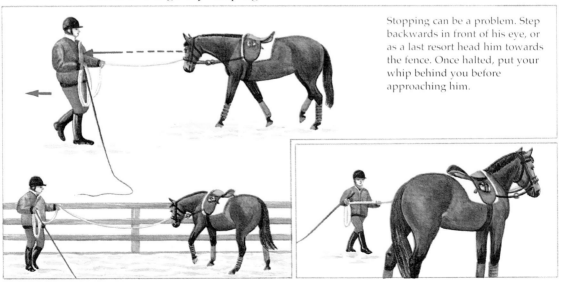

Stopping can be a problem. Step backwards in front of his eye, or as a last resort head him towards the fence. Once halted, put your whip behind you before approaching him.

Lungeing the Young Horse

You must be proficient at lungeing a trained horse before you attempt to teach a young horse to lunge.

Lungeing is the introduction to training for the young horse. The youngster which has been well handled and taught to lead correctly from the start is not usually a problem. Teach him to go forward when he is led. The handler should be able to stay level with the horse's shoulder whilst the horse walks actively forwards without pulling. Use the same voice commands that you intend to use for lungeing: 'walk-on' and 'whoa'. Lead him from both sides – it is amazing the lengths to which a horse will go to get his handler back on his near side, simply because he is not used to him being on his off-side.

When lungeing for the first few times, use just a lungeing cavesson with the lunge rein attached to the middle ring. If your youngster is particularly strong and wilful you may need to establish control by putting a snaffle bit in his mouth and attaching the lunge rein through the bit and over his head (see page 15). Avoid doing this where possible as you do not want to damage his mouth or make him afraid of the bit.

Always start this early lungeing in an enclosed area with good footing.

There are two methods of teaching the horse to lunge:

1. Ask an assistant to lead the horse whilst you stand in the middle giving the appropriate commands until the horse understands. Your assistant must be efficient or he could easily get in the way and even get kicked.

2. It is usually more practical to lead the horse on a circle on the left rein, gradually allowing him to take the rein longer whilst sending him forwards with your voice and gentle use of the whip. If he breaks into trot at this stage, don't stop him; allow him out onto a bigger circle and encourage him quietly forwards.

Once he knows to move away from you and stay out on the circle on the left rein, repeat the process on the right rein.

The position of your body in relation to the horse is important. Do not get in front of his eye or he may stop and turn in. This can produce a confrontation and should be avoided. Try to stay in a 'driving' position, slightly behind his girth but out of reach of his hind legs. Keep him looking to the inside so that if he does kick out, he cannot kick you.

Above all, do your utmost not to let him go if he should try to pull away from you. A loose, frightened horse, with the lunge rein dangling, can cause a serious accident.

A horse which has been trained to lead well will usually lunge well.

Make sure that the horse walks away from you.

Get level with his quarters and send him forwards in front of you. Take care to avoid being kicked by keeping his head turned to the inside.

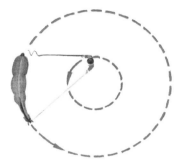

The 'driving' position from above.

It is good if he will stretch his head down and move actively forward.

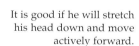

Always repeat everything on both reins, but expect more difficulty with the young horse on the right rein.

Problems and Solutions

Incorrect bend on the circle

Most horses prefer to lean in towards the centre of the circle, putting their weight on their inside shoulder and looking to the outside. Whilst doing this they also drop the contact on the lunge rein. Encourage the horse to take more of a contact by pointing or flicking the whip towards his shoulder; use the command 'Keep out'. Make sure that when he does meet the rein contact he finds it elastic and doesn't get a jolt on his nose. You may have to work him on a smaller circle in walk to begin with. Once you have a contact, 'take and give' on the lunge rein to encourage him to look to the inside, whilst pushing him away from you with the whip at his shoulder. Side-reins help to keep him correctly bent by encouraging him to take a contact with the outside rein. In cases of extreme stiffness you can make the inside side-rein shorter, forcing the horse to bend his neck. This is only a short-term way to make a breakthrough, as it will encourage him to escape through his outside shoulder and lean on the side-rein.

Falling out

This is where the horse tries to make the circle bigger than you want by bending his neck and putting his weight onto his outside shoulder. Often the horse that bends incorrectly on one rein will 'fall out' on the other. The horse evades engaging his hind legs as they will swing out instead of stepping under his body. Side-reins will prevent this by controlling the amount of bend in the neck.

Turning in to face you

When this happens it is necessary to go up to the horse and start again. It is essential that you keep him moving forwards. Side-reins will help you to control him. Stay slightly behind him – you will need to walk in order to be in position to keep him moving. When you ask him to halt, make him do so without turning in. You may have to spend some time on this but it will pay off in the end.

Shying

If your horse is the 'spooky' type he will probably shy on the lunge. The correction is the same as for when he goes with the wrong bend: make him take a contact and flick the whip towards his shoulder. Try to anticipate when he is going to shy and exaggerate the bend to the inside, pointing the whip at his shoulder.

Being lazy

The horse should make upward transitions from the voice alone, however you will need to back up this with the lunge whip if he is lazy. If he does not react to the voice and a 'flick' of the whip, then give him a sharp smack just above his hocks. Be prepared for him to shoot forwards. Try not to pull him up too sharply as you do not wish to discourage any forward movement.

Running away

If the horse decides to take off, take the rein in both hands and lean back with your weight braced on your heels. Either drop the whip or, preferably, keep it behind you. In an indoor school, you can run him into the wall, but do not run him into anything that he might jump. If you know that the horse is strong or fresh, then attach the lunge rein to the bit, as shown, before you start. Do your utmost not to let him go as a loose horse with a lunge rein dangling can cause a serious accident.

TURNING IN TO FACE YOU

Go up to him and start again making sure that you keep him going forwards and that he doesn't have the chance to stop and turn in again.

SHYING

Push him out into the contact by pointing and using the whip towards his shoulder. Try to keep an inside bend, turning his head away from what he is shying at.

 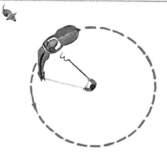

REFUSING TO MOVE / LAZINESS

Here your voice commands need to be reinforced with a sharp reminder with the whip.

RUNNING AWAY

For extra control, put the lunge rein through the bit and over his head, buckling it to the bit on the other side.

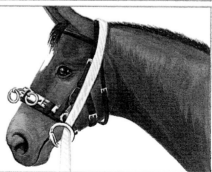

Trotting Poles

Lungeing over trotting poles is an excellent gymnastic exercise. It can help to improve the rhythm and outline whilst encouraging the horse to flex his joints.

Before attempting pole work, the horse must lunge well, take a good contact and stay out on the circle. He should wear a lunge cavesson, brushing boots and overreach boots.

Start by placing a single pole on the track, against the wall on the long side. Lead him over this on each rein until he is perfectly relaxed. Then work him on a circle, away from the pole until he is settled and warmed up. Make his approach to the pole in walk, allowing him to make some straight strides in front of and after the pole. It is necessary for you to walk with him for those few straight strides. He may jump the pole, so be prepared to go with him. If he gets lively, circle him away until he is calm.

Once the horse will walk calmly over the pole, repeat the exercise in trot. Ideally he should lower his head and neck and maintain his rhythm. When this has been achieved, you can add two more poles. They should be 1.35m (4'6") apart for the average-striding horse, but adjust up or down to suit – the hind foot should land exactly half way between the poles. Using poles in a fan shape will develop the flexion of his inside hind leg.

FIRST ATTEMPT

APPROACH TOO SHARP

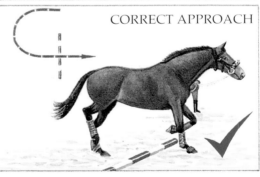

CORRECT APPROACH

FAN OF POLES When working over poles on a circle the horse is constantly turning and therefore has to flex his joints and use himself well to negotiate the exercise. Keep him to the middle of the poles.

Distance through the middle – 1.35m / 4'6"

16

Jumping

Working a young horse over fences on the lunge can serve as a good introduction to jumping. He will learn to leave the ground without the added complication of having a rider's weight on his back. If a horse develops a problem with his jumping then lungeing him over a fence can help to diagnose where the fault lies.

Once he has mastered trotting over a single pole, then he is ready to jump small fences. The use of lines of trotting poles can take away the horse's natural reaction to jump, and he may try to trot over small fences when he is first introduced to them. For this reason it is better not to mix trotting pole work with jumping in the early stages.

The fence should be positioned against the wall of the school, making sure that there is plenty of room for him to take a straight approach and landing. Great care should be taken in the building of the fence. The wing on the inside must not be higher than the fence itself or the lunge rein will snag on it. Using a guide rail will prevent this and help to stop the horse running out. Plastic jump blocks (Bloks) are good to use as wings when lungeing. It is very helpful to have an assistant to alter the fence as necessary.

Start by leading the horse between the wings so that he knows the way through. Place one end of the pole at a low height on the inside wing. You can then quietly work the horse in trot over the fence. Be prepared to go with him on the landing side and take great care not to get in front of his eye on the approach – you could put him off and then he might stop. If he takes off bucking on the landing side, go with him for a few strides and then bring him quite sharply onto a circle. Wait until he has settled again before working your

Have a pole resting on the fence to prevent the lunge rein getting caught. It will also help to guide the horse to the middle of the fence.

Jumping (continued)

way back up the school to make another approach. Always repeat the exercise on the other rein. Once the horse pops over confidently and calmly, make the fence into a cross pole. You can then progress to a small spread, or add a placing pole, whatever you feel will improve his technique. Take care not to overface him as it will ruin his confidence.

Dealing with a refusal

If he does stop, try not to let him turn away from the fence. Ask your assistant to dismantle the fence in front of him and then lead him through. Reduce the height of the fence and then try again. It is important that he does not learn to whip round in front of the fence.

Try to analyse why the refusal happened in the first place. Have you made the fence too big? Is the going unsuitable? Is he going forwards enough before the fence? Were you careful enough with your own position, and did you have him straight enough in front of the fence? Is the horse sound or is something hurting him? There are many possible reasons. Making the correction is so much easier if you understand the cause.

Once you have eliminated all the causes you may come to the conclusion that the horse is not frightened but just being naughty. In this case you will need to be firm with him and encourage him with the lunge whip as soon as he hesitates. Always make sure that you finish on a good note, even if it means reducing the size of the fence to get him jumping freely again.

Lungeing for Exercise

When time and labour are in short supply, lungeing can take the place of ridden work on two or three days each week. This can be especially useful during the winter months when daylight hours are short. However, you cannot use lungeing alone to achieve or maintain fitness. The constant turning can strain the joints and it can be monotonous.

Provided the horse is obedient, it is quite acceptable to lunge with just brushing boots and a cavesson, lunge rein and whip. However, most horses will work better with a bridle and side-reins attached to a saddle or roller.

The horse must be made to work actively forwards on as big a circle as possible in walk, trot and, if circumstances allow, canter. Build up gradually from 8 minutes on each rein with equal amounts of walk and trot, to a maximum of 40 minutes, with the horse cantering for several 3-minute periods. Always do less rather than too much.

To maintain the horse's fitness for riding club, dressage and show jumping activities, 25-30 minutes will be plenty. For hunting and one-day eventing, you will need to give him 30-40 minutes, depending on the other work that you are able to give him during the week.

Always include plenty of walking, using the walk periods as recovery time, as one would for interval training. Allow the horse's respiration rate to return to normal before working again at a faster pace.

In the winter months, if your artificial surface freezes and you want to keep the horse working, you can put down straw or manure in a 20m circle on the grass and lunge the horse on this. However, this won't do your grass much good!

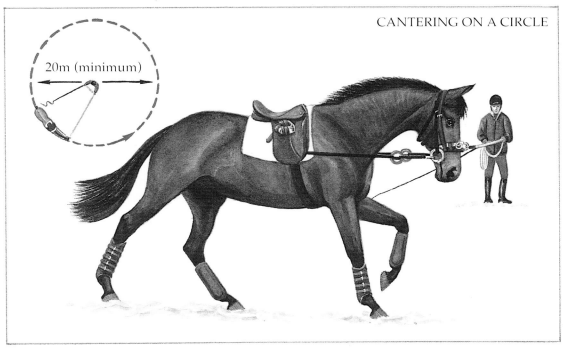

CANTERING ON A CIRCLE

20m (minimum)

Training Aids

Training aids can be valuable in helping to establish a contact with the horse's mouth and in inviting him to go in a correct outline. There are various types available, three of which are outlined here. Whatever type you choose, though, always start with it very loose and shorten it progressively once the horse is confident with its action and effect.

The Lauffer rein

Named after its inventor, this consists of two reins. One rein is attached on each side to the bit and to the lower and middle rings on the roller. The effect here is to encourage the horse to take his head forwards and down. It is less restricting than side-reins and encourages the horse to work more through his back. Once the horse is familiar with its effect and works well in a forward and down outline, the rein can be moved onto the middle and higher rings. This will encourage him to come up a little more in front, allowing him to come off his forehand and to take more weight on his hind legs.

The Chambon

This consists of a strap attached to the girth between the front legs, which then divides, going up to a headpiece where it threads through rings on either side and then attaches to the bit.

When the horse raises his head, the bit comes into contact with the corners of his mouth and creates pressure on his poll. When the horse lowers his head this pressure is released. The horse soon learns to stretch his neck down and forward. This, when used in conjunction with actively engaged hind legs, will develop strength and suppleness in his back.

The disadvantage of the Chambon is

that it does not stabilise the neck at the withers and can encourage the horse to fall out through his shoulder by bending too much in his neck. This will limit the amount that you can effectively engage his hind legs. However, it is an excellent aid to help horses which have been injured or are just very stiff in their backs.

Side-reins

Side-reins are the most common and conventional of the training aids. Correctly used they encourage the horse to go forwards into the bridle, to relax the jaw and to flex at the poll. Side-reins invite the horse to take a contact with the bit; they also teach him that he must respect the bit and not pull against it. They prevent him from falling out through the shoulder, therefore helping to make him straight and encouraging him to go into the outside rein.

Problems can occur if the side-reins are fitted too tightly: the horse may panic and run backwards, he may even rear up and could go over backwards. If the horse is allowed to be inactive, he could learn to drop the bit and evade the contact altogether. The side-reins should always be fitted so that they are level on either side and at the same height as the horse's mouth when he is working in a correct outline. (See also page 7.)

When the horse works well, going forwards into the bridle with correct bend on the circle, the inside side-rein will become loose and the horse will work clearly forwards into the outside rein. He will be relaxed in his poll, and his mouth will be moist as he accepts the bit. His inside hind leg will step forwards under his body, and he will be working in a correct way, developing the right muscles.

LAUFFER REIN

The horse is not held in a fixed position; he may move his head up or down and the contact will be maintained.

CHAMBON

Pressure is applied at the poll as well as on the lips and corners of the mouth.

SIDE-REINS

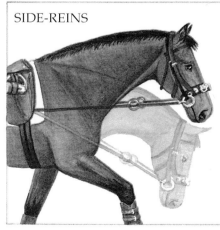

The horse can raise and lower his head but can also learn to come behind the bit. Side-reins encourage a contact with the outside rein.

More Advanced Work

Lungeing for improvement

Lungeing can be a very useful aid in diagnosing the cause of any problems that occur when ridden. For example, if the horse tilts his head when ridden but is level on the lunge, then the rider must look to correcting his own position. This is particularly useful when looking at problems in the mouth: if they are not there when the horse is on the lunge, then the cause must be either the rider's hands or pain in the back.

Lungeing can be most beneficial in the retraining of spoilt horses. Horses which have learnt to go in a hollow outline have developed the wrong muscles and are not carrying their riders in the most efficient way. The correct muscles have to be built up gradually. Most horses will put up a lot of resistance to this and it is far better that they argue with themselves on the lunge without the added handicap of the rider's weight. Progressive work using the training aids described earlier will encourage long-term improvement.

Variations within the pace

You can work to improve the horse's ability to lengthen and shorten his stride both in trot and canter. Once he maintains his balance and rhythm in working paces and is obedient to the voice, he is ready to vary the pace. Start by making a few straight strides down the long side of the area that you are working in. You will need to walk with him. Once he understands that you want him to go straight and will keep a good contact, you can ask for some lengthening. Depending on how forward-thinking he is, you may just need to 'click' at him, or if he is lazy you may need to flick him with the lunge whip. Try to keep him in a good rhythm and only ask for a few

HOLLOW

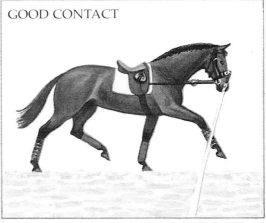

GOOD CONTACT

EXTENDED TROT

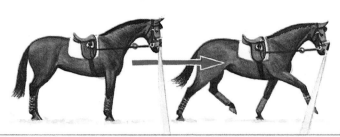

DIRECT TRANSITION (HALT TO TROT)

Direct transitions can be encouraged to help make the horse more responsive and engaged.

strides to begin with. The most likely problem is that he will break into canter or 'run' with short, hurried steps. In both cases bring him back to a working trot and then try again. Try to use your voice in time with the rhythm of the trot.

Asking for longer steps in the canter is done in the same way. Here the most common problem is that the horse may become over-excited. If that happens, bring him back to trot and wait until he is calm before trying again. You can develop this work by asking for longer steps on the circle.

Transitions

When you first start working the horse on the lunge, you cannot expect him to react very quickly when asked to make a transition from one pace to another. Once he is more tuned in to what you are asking, the transitions can be more direct. For example, you can ask him to go from halt directly into trot, and from canter into walk. These transitions will help to engage his hind legs and make him stronger – but be careful to keep him thinking forwards, especially in the downward transitions.

Lateral work

You can lay the foundations for basic lateral work by decreasing and increasing the size of the circle. Begin this exercise in walk, shortening the lunge rein to bring him onto a smaller circle. In walk he can manage as small as 6m. Then pointing the whip at his rib cage, push him out to the bigger circle. He should step sideways, his inside hind leg moving in front of and across his outside hind leg. Repeat this exercise in trot, maintain the bend to the inside so that his inside hind leg has to flex and take more weight as it comes under his body. Repeat this exercise on both reins.

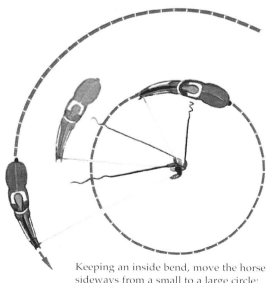

Keeping an inside bend, move the horse sideways from a small to a large circle; this again helps with the flexion of the hind legs.

23

Ten Golden Rules

1. Always wear gloves when handling a lunge rein.

2. Make sure that the surface on which you intend to lunge is suitable.

3. Always coil your lunge rein yourself.

4. Do not drop your lunge whip on the ground.

5. Protect your horse's legs with boots or bandages.

6. Do not over-tighten the side-reins.

7. Make sure that the circle is big enough.

8. Work equally on both reins.

9. Lungeing is tiring for the horse; do only as much as his fitness will allow.

10. Never take chances, especially with a horse that you do not know.